The Chinese Nightingale and Other Poems

By

Vachel Lindsay Vachel

Published by Forgotten Books 2012

Originally Published 1919

PIBN 1000360953

THE CHINESE NIGHTINGALE
AND OTHER POEMS

THE MACMILLAN COMPANY
NEW YORK · BOSTON · CHICAGO · DALLAS
ATLANTA · SAN FRANCISCO

MACMILLAN & CO., Limited
LONDON · BOMBAY · CALCUTTA
MELBOURNE

THE MACMILLAN CO. OF CANADA, Ltd.
TORONTO

THE

CHINESE NIGHTINGALE

AND OTHER POEMS

BY

Nicholas VACHEL LINDSAY

AUTHOR OF "THE CONGO," "GENERAL WILLIAM BOOTH ENTERS
INTO HEAVEN," "ADVENTURES WHILE PREACHING
THE GOSPEL OF BEAUTY," ETC.

New York
THE MACMILLAN COMPANY
1919

Norwood Press
J. S. Cushing Co. — Berwick & Smith Co.
Norwood, Mass., U.S.A.

THIS BOOK IS DEDICATED TO
SARA TEASDALE, POET

The thanks of the author is extended to "Poetry : A Magazine of Verse," "The Chicago Herald," "The Masses," "The Red Cross Magazine," "The Bookman," "The Seven Arts," "The Independent," "The Forum," and "Tuck's Magazine" for permission to reprint many of the verses in this volume.

Harriet Monroe awarded the Levinson Prize to "The Chinese Nightingale," as the best contribution to "Poetry : A Magazine of Verse," for the year 1915.

TABLE OF CONTENTS

FIRST SECTION

SECOND SECTION

America Watching the War, August, 1914, to April, 1917

THIRD SECTION

America at War with Germany, Beginning April, 1917

FOURTH SECTION

Tragedies, Comedies and Dreams

FIFTH SECTION

The Poem Games

FIRST SECTION

THE CHINESE NIGHTINGALE

THE CHINESE NIGHTINGALE

A Song in Chinese Tapestries

"How, how," he said.   "Friend Chang," I said,
"San Francisco sleeps as the dead —
Ended license, lust and play:
Why do you iron the night away?
Your big clock speaks with a deadly sound,
With a tick and a wail till dawn comes round.
While the monster shadows glower and creep,
What can be better for man than sleep?"

"I will tell you a secret," Chang replied;
"My breast with vision is satisfied,
And I see green trees and fluttering wings,
And my deathless bird from Shanghai sings."
Then he lit five fire-crackers in a pan.
"Pop, pop," said the fire-crackers, "cra-cra-crack.'
He lit a joss stick long and black.
Then the proud gray joss in the corner stirred;
On his wrist appeared a gray small bird,
And this was the song of the gray small bird:

3

"Where is the princess, loved forever,
Who made Chang first of the kings of men?"

And the joss in the corner stirred again;
And the carved dog, curled in his arms, awoke,
Barked forth a smoke-cloud that whirled and broke.
It piled in a maze round the ironing-place,
And there on the snowy table wide
Stood a Chinese lady of high degree,
With a scornful, witching, tea-rose face. . . .
Yet she put away all form and pride,
And laid her glimmering veil aside
With a childlike smile for Chang and for me.

The walls fell back, night was aflower,
The table gleamed in a moonlit bower,
While Chang, with a countenance carved of stone,
Ironed and ironed, all alone.
And thus she sang to the busy man Chang:
"Have you forgotten. . . .
Deep in the ages, long, long ago,
I was your sweetheart, there on the sand —
Storm-worn beach of the Chinese land?
We sold our grain in the peacock town
Built on the edge of the sea-sands brown —
Built on the edge of the sea-sands brown. . . .

"When all the world was drinking blood
From the skulls of men and bulls
And all the world had swords and clubs of stone,
We drank our tea in China beneath the sacred spice-trees,
And heard the curled waves of the harbor moan.
And this gray bird, in Love's first spring,
With a bright-bronze breast and a bronze-brown wing,
Captured the world with his carolling.
Do you remember, ages after,
At last the world we were born to own?
You were the heir of the yellow throne —
The world was the field of the Chinese man
And we were the pride of the Sons of Han?
We copied deep books and we carved in jade,
And wove blue silks in the mulberry shade. . . ."

"I remember, I remember
That Spring came on forever,
That Spring came on forever,"
Said the Chinese nightingale.

My heart was filled with marvel and dream,
Though I saw the western street-lamps gleam,
Though dawn was bringing the western day,
Though Chang was a laundryman ironing away. . . .

Mingled there with the streets and alleys,
The railroad-yard and the clock-tower bright,
Demon clouds crossed ancient valleys;
Across wide lotus-ponds of light
I marked a giant firefly's flight.

And the lady, rosy-red,
Flourished her fan, her shimmering fan,
Stretched her hand toward Chang, and said:
"Do you remember,
Ages after,
Our palace of heart-red stone?
Do you remember
The little doll-faced children
With their lanterns full of moon-fire,
That came from all the empire
Honoring the throne? —
The loveliest fête and carnival
Our world had ever known?
The sages sat about us
With their heads bowed in their beards,
With proper meditation on the sight.
Confucius was not born;
We lived in those great days
Confucius later said were lived aright. . . .

THE CHINESE NIGHTINGALE

And this gray bird, on that day of spring,
With a bright bronze breast, and a bronze-brown wing,
Captured the world with his carolling.
Late at night his tune was spent.
Peasants,
Sages,
Children,
Homeward went,
And then the bronze bird sang for you and me.
We walked alone.   Our hearts were high and free.
I had a silvery name, I had a silvery name,
I had a silvery name — do you remember
The name you cried beside the tumbling sea?"

Chang turned not to the lady slim —
He bent to his work, ironing away;
But she was arch, and knowing and glowing,
And the bird on his shoulder spoke for him.

"Darling . . . darling . . . darling . . . darling . . ."
Said the Chinese nightingale.

The great gray joss on a rustic shelf,
Rakish and shrewd, with his collar awry,
Sang impolitely, as though by himself,

Drowning with his bellowing the nightingale's cry:
"Back through a hundred, hundred years
Hear the waves as they climb the piers,
Hear the howl of the silver seas,
Hear the thunder.
Hear the gongs of holy China
How the waves and tunes combine
In a rhythmic clashing wonder,
Incantation old and fine:
   'Dragons, dragons, Chinese dragons,
   Red fire-crackers, and green fire-crackers,
   And dragons, dragons, Chinese dragons.'"

Then the lady, rosy-red,
Turned to her lover Chang and said:
"Dare you forget that turquoise dawn
When we stood in our mist-hung velvet lawn,
And worked a spell this great joss taught
Till a God of the Dragons was charmed and caught?
From the flag high over our palace home
He flew to our feet in rainbow-foam —
A king of beauty and tempest and thunder
Panting to tear our sorrows asunder.
A dragon of fair adventure and wonder.
We mounted the back of that royal slave

With thoughts of desire that were noble and grave.
We swam down the shore to the dragon-mountains,
We whirled to the peaks and the fiery fountains.
To our secret ivory house we were bourne.
We looked down the wonderful wing-filled regions
Where the dragons darted in glimmering legions.
Right by my breast the nightingale sang;
The old rhymes rang in the sunlit mist
That we this hour regain —
Song-fire for the brain.
When my hands and my hair and my feet you kissed,
When you cried for your heart's new pain,
What was my name in the dragon-mist,
In the rings of rainbowed rain?"

"Sorrow and love, glory and love," i
Said the Chinese nightingale.
"Sorrow and love, glory and love,"
Said the Chinese nightingale.

And now the joss broke in with his song:
"Dying ember, bird of Chang,
Soul of Chang, do you remember? —
Ere you returned to the shining harbor
There were pirates by ten thousand

Descended on the town
In vessels mountain-high and red and brown,
Moon-ships that climbed the storms and cut the skies.
On their prows were painted terrible bright eyes.
But I was then a wizard and a scholar and a priest;
I stood upon the sand;   .
With lifted hand I looked upon them
And sunk their vessels with my wizard eyes,
And the stately lacquer-gate made safe again.
Deep, deep below the bay, the sea-weed and the spray,
Embalmed in amber every pirate lies,
Embalmed in amber every pirate lies."

Then this did the noble lady say:
"Bird, do you dream of our home-coming day
When you flew like a courier on before
From the dragon-peak to our palace-door,
And we drove the steed in your singing path —
The ramping dragon of laughter and wrath:
And found our city all aglow,
And knighted this joss that decked it so?
There were golden fishes in the purple river
And silver fishes and rainbow fishes.
There were golden junks in the laughing river,
And silver junks and rainbow junks:

There were golden lilies by the bay and river,
And silver lilies and tiger-lilies,
And tinkling wind-bells in the gardens of the town
By the black-lacquer gate
Where walked in state
The kind king Chang
And his sweet-heart mate. . . .
With his flag-born dragon
And his crown of pearl . . . and . . . jade,
And his nightingale reigning in the mulberry shade,
And sailors and soldiers on the sea-sands brown,
And priests who bowed them down to your song —
By the city called Han, the peacock town,
By the city called Han, the nightingale town,
The nightingale town."

Then sang the bird, so strangely gay,
Fluttering, fluttering, ghostly and gray,
A vague, unravelling, final tune,
Like a long unwinding silk cocoon ;
Sang as though for the soul of him
Who ironed away in that bower dim : —
    "I have forgotten
    Your dragons great,
    Merry and mad and friendly and bold.

Dim is your proud lost palace-gate.

I vaguely know

There were heroes of old,

Troubles more than the heart could hold,

There were wolves in the woods

Yet lambs in the fold,

Nests in the top of the almond tree. . . .

The evergreen tree . . . and the mulberry tree

Life and hurry and joy forgotten,

Years on years I but half-remember . . .

Man is a torch, then ashes soon,

May and June, then dead December,

Dead December, then again June.

Who shall end my dream's confusion?

Life is a loom, weaving illusion . . .

I remember, I remember

There were ghostly veils and laces . . .

In the shadowy bowery places . . .

With lovers' ardent faces

Bending to one another,

Speaking each his part.

They infinitely echo

In the red cave of my heart.

'Sweetheart, sweetheart, sweetheart.'

They said to one another.

They spoke, I think, of perils past.
They spoke, I think, of peace at last.
One thing I remember :
Spring came on forever,
Spring came on forever,"
Said the Chinese nightingale.

SECOND SECTION

AMERICA WATCHING THE WAR
AUGUST, 1914 TO APRIL, 1917

WHERE IS THE REAL NON-RESISTANT?

(Matthew V, 38–48.)

Who can surrender to Christ, dividing his best with the
 stranger,
Giving to each what he asks, braving the uttermost
 danger
All for the enemy, MAN?   Who can surrender till death
His words and his works, his house and his lands,
His eyes and his heart and his breath?

Who can surrender to Christ?   Many have yearned
 toward it daily.
Yet they surrender to passion, wildly or grimly or
 gaily;
Yet they surrender to pride, counting her precious and
 queenly;
Yet they surrender to knowledge, preening their feathers
 serenely.

Who can surrender to Christ?   Where is the man so
 transcendent,

c   17

So heated with love of his kind, so filled with the spirit
    resplendent
That all of the hours of his day his song is thrilling and
    tender,
And all of his thoughts to our white cause of peace
        Surrender, surrender, surrender?

HERE'S TO THE MICE

(Written with the hope that the socialists might yet dethrone Kaiser and Czar.)

Here's to the mice that scare the lions,
Creeping into their cages.
Here's to the fairy mice that bite
The elephants fat and wise :
Hidden in the hay-pile while the elephant thunder rages.
Here's to the scurrying, timid mice
Through whom the proud cause dies.

Here's to the seeming accident
When all is planned and working,
All the flywheels turning,
Not a vassal shirking.
Here's to the hidden tunneling thing
That brings the mountain's groans.
Here's to the midnight scamps that gnaw,
Gnawing away the thrones.

WHEN BRYAN SPEAKS

When Bryan speaks, the town's a hive.
From miles around, the autos drive.
The sparrow chirps.   The rooster crows.
The place is kicking and alive.

When Bryan speaks, the bunting glows.
The raw procession onward flows.
The small dogs bark.   The children laugh
A wind of springtime fancy blows.

When Bryan speaks, the wigwam shakes.
The corporation magnate quakes.
The pre-convention plot is smashed.
The valiant pleb full-armed awakes.

When Bryan speaks, the sky is ours,
The wheat, the forests, and the flowers.
And who is here to say us nay?
Fled are the ancient tyrant powers.

When Bryan speaks, then I rejoice.

His is the strange composite voice

Of many million singing souls

Who make world-brotherhood their choice.

Written in WASHINGTON, D.C.
February, 1915.

TO JANE ADDAMS AT THE HAGUE

Two Poems, written on the Sinking of the Lusitania.
Appearing in the Chicago *Herald*, May 11, 1915.

I. SPEAK NOW FOR PEACE

Lady of Light, and our best woman, and queen,
Stand now for peace, (though anger breaks your heart),
Though naught but smoke and flame and drowning is seen.

Lady of Light, speak, though you speak alone,
Though your voice may seem as a dove's in this howling
    flood,
It is heard to-night by every senate and throne.

Though the widening battle of millions and millions of men
Threatens to-night to sweep the whole of the earth,
Back of the smoke is the promise of kindness again.

II. TOLSTOI IS PLOWING YET

Tolstoi is plowing yet.   When the smoke-clouds break,
High in the sky shines a field as wide as the world.
There he toils for the Kingdom of Heaven's sake.

Ah, he is taller than clouds of the little earth.
Only the congress of planets is over him,
And the arching path where new sweet stars have birth.

Wearing his peasant dress, his head bent low,
Tolstoi, that angel of Peace, is plowing yet;
Forward, across the field, his horses go.

THE TALE OF THE TIGER TREE

A Fantasy, dedicated to the little poet Alice Oliver Henderson, ten years old.

The Fantasy shows how tiger-hearts are the cause of war in all ages. It shows how the mammoth forces may be either friends or enemies of the struggle for peace. It shows how the dream of peace is unconquerable and eternal.

I

Peace-of-the-Heart, my own for long,
Whose shining hair the May-winds fan,
Making it tangled as they can,
A mystery still, star-shining yet,
Through ancient ages known to me
And now once more reborn with me: —

This is the tale of the Tiger Tree
A hundred times the height of a man,
Lord of the race since the world began.

This is my city Springfield,
My home on the breast of the plain.

THE TALE OF THE TIGER TREE

The state house towers to heaven,
By an arsenal gray as the rain . . .
And suddenly all is mist,
And I walk in a world apart,
In the forest-age when I first knelt down
At your feet, O Peace-of-the-Heart.

This is the wonder of twilight :
Three times as high as the dome
Tiger-striped trees encircle the town,
Golden geysers of foam.
While giant white parrots sail past in their pride.
The roofs now are clouds and storms that they ride.
And there with the huntsmen of mound-builder days
Through jungle and meadow I stride.
And the Tiger Tree leaf is falling around
As it fell when the world began :
Like a monstrous tiger-skin, stretched on the ground,
Or the cloak of a medicine man.
A deep-crumpled gossamer web,
Fringed with the fangs of a snake.
The wind swirls it down from the leperous boughs.
It shimmers on clay-hill and lake,
With the gleam of great bubbles of blood,
Or coiled like a rainbow shell. . . .

I feast on the stem of the Leaf as I march.
I am burning with Heaven and Hell.

II

The gray king died in his hour.
Then we crowned you, the prophetess wise:
Peace-of-the-Heart we deeply adored
For the witchcraft hid in your eyes.
Gift from the sky, overmastering all,
You sent forth your magical parrots to call
The plot-hatching prince of the tigers,
To your throne by the red-clay wall.

Thus came that genius insane:
Spitting and slinking,
Sneering and vain,
He sprawled to your grassy throne, drunk on The Leaf,
The drug that was cunning and splendor and grief.
He had fled from the mammoth by day,
He had blasted the mammoth by night,
War was his drunkenness,
War was his dreaming,
War was his love and his play.
And he hissed at your heavenly glory
While his councillors snarled in delight,

Asking in irony : "What shall we learn
From this whisperer, fragile and white?"

And had you not been an enchantress
They would not have loitered to mock
Nor spared your white parrots who walked by their paws
With bantering venturesome talk.

You made a white fire of The Leaf.
You sang while the tiger-chiefs hissed.
You chanted of "Peace to the wonderful world."
And they saw you in dazzling mist.
And their steps were no longer insane,
Kindness came down like the rain,
They dreamed that like fleet young ponies they feasted
On succulent grasses and grain.

.   .   .   .

Then came the black-mammoth chief :
Long-haired and shaggy and great,
Proud and sagacious he marshalled his court :
(You had sent him your parrots of state.)
His trunk in rebellion upcurled,
A curse at the tiger he hurled.
Huge elephants trumpeted there by his side,

And mastodon-chiefs of the world.

But higher magic began.

For the turbulent vassals of man.

You harnessed their fever, you conquered their ire,

Their hearts turned to flowers through holy desire,

For their darling and star you were crowned,

And their raging demons were bound.

You rode on the back of the yellow-streaked king,

His loose neck was wreathed with a mistletoe ring.

Primordial elephants loomed by your side,

And our clay-painted children danced by your path,

Chanting the death of the kingdoms of wrath.

You wrought until night with us all.

The fierce brutes fawned at your call,

Then slipped to their lairs, song-chained.

And thus you sang sweetly, and reigned:

"Immortal is the inner peace, free to beasts and men.

Beginning in the darkness, the mystery will conquer,

And now it comforts every heart that seeks for love
again.

And now the mammoth bows the knee,

We hew down every Tiger Tree,

We send each tiger bound in love and glory to his den,

Bound in love . . . and wisdom . . . and glory, . . . to
his den."

III

"Beware of the trumpeting swine,"
Came the howl from the northward that night.
Twice-rebel tigers warning was still
If we held not beside them it boded us ill.
From the parrots translating the cry,
And the apes in the trees came the whine:
"Beware of the trumpeting swine.
Beware of the faith of a mammoth."

"Beware of the faith of a tiger,"
Came the roar from the southward that night.
Trumpeting mammoths warning us still
If we held not beside them it boded us ill.
The frail apes wailed to us all,
The parrots reechoed the call:
"Beware of the faith of a tiger."
From the heights of the forest the watchers could see
The tiger-cats crunching the Leaf of the Tree
Lashing themselves, and scattering foam,
Killing our huntsmen, hurrying home.
The chiefs of the mammoths our mastery spurned,
And eastward restlessly fumed and burned.
The peacocks squalled out the news of their drilling
And told how they trampled, maneuvered, and turned.

Ten thousand man-hating tigers
Whirling down from the north, like a flood!
Ten thousand mammoths oncoming
From the south as avengers of blood!
Our child-queen was mourning, her magic was dead,
The roots of the Tiger Tree reeking with red.

IV

This is the tale of the Tiger Tree
A hundred times the height of a man,
Lord of the race since the world began.

We marched to the mammoths,
We pledged them our steel,
And scorning you, sang: —
"We are men,
We are men."
We mounted their necks,
And they stamped a wide reel.
We sang:
"We are fighting the hell-cats again,
We are mound-builder men,
We are elephant men."
We left you there, lonely,

Beauty your power,
Wisdom your watchman,
To hold the clay tower.
While the black-mammoths boomed —
"You are elephant men,
Men,
Men,
Elephant men."
The dawn-winds prophesied battles untold.
While the Tiger Trees roared of the glories of old,
Of the masterful spirits and hard.

The drunken cats came in their joy
In the sunrise, a glittering wave.
"We are tigers, are tigers," they yowled.
"Down,
Down,
Go the swine to the grave."
But we tramp
Tramp
Trampled them there,
Then charged with our sabres and spears.
The swish of the sabre,
The swish of the sabre,
Was a marvellous tune in our ears.

We yelled "We are men,
We are men."
As we bled to death in the sun. . . .
Then staunched our horrible wounds
With the cry that the battle was won. . . .
And at last,
When the black-mammoth legion
Split the night with their song : —
"Right is braver than wrong,
Right is stronger than wrong,"
The buzzards came taunting :
"Down from the north
Tiger-nations are sweeping along."

.   .   .   .   .   .

Then we ate of the ravening Leaf
As our savage fathers of old.
No longer our wounds made us weak,
No longer our pulses were cold.
Though half of my troops were afoot,
(For the great who had borne them were slain)
We dreamed we were tigers, and leaped
And foamed with that vision insane.
We cried "We are soldiers of doom,
Doom,

Sabres of glory and doom."
We wreathed the king of the mammoths
In the tiger-leaves' terrible bloom.
We flattered the king of the mammoths,
Loud-rattling sabres and spears.
The swish of the sabre,
The swish of the sabre,
Was a marvellous tune in his ears.

v

This was the end of the battle.
The tigers poured by in a tide
Over us all with their caterwaul call,
"We are the tigers,"
They cried.
"We are the sabres,"
They cried.
But we laughed while our blades swept wide,
While the dawn-rays stabbed through the gloom.
"We are suns on fire" was our yell —
"Suns on fire." . . .
But man-child and mastodon fell,
Mammoth and elephant fell.
The fangs of the devil-cats closed on the world,
Plunged it to blackness and doom.

The desolate red-clay wall
Echoed the parrots' call : —
"Immortal is the inner peace, free to beasts and men.
Beginning in the darkness, the mystery will conquer,
And now it comforts every heart that seeks for love again.
And now the mammoth bows the knee,
We hew down every Tiger Tree,
We send each tiger bound in love and glory to his den,
Bound in love . . . and wisdom . . . and glory, . . . to
    his den."

A peacock screamed of his beauty
On that broken wall by the trees,
Chiding his little mate,
Spreading his fans in the breeze . . .
And you, with eyes of a bride,
Knelt on the wall at my side,
The deathless song in your mouth . . .
A million new tigers swept south . . .
As we laughed at the peacock, and died.

This is my vision in Springfield :
Three times as high as the dome,
Tiger-striped trees encircle the town,
Golden geysers of foam ; —
Though giant white parrots sail past, giving voice,
Though I walk with Peace-of-the-Heart and rejoice.

THE MERCIFUL HAND

Written to Miss Alice L. F. Fitzgerald, Edith Cavell
memorial nurse, going to the front.

Your fine white hand is Heaven's gift
To cure the wide world, stricken sore,
Bleeding at the breast and head,
Tearing at its wounds once more.

Your white hand is a prophecy,
A living hope that Christ shall come
And make the nations merciful,
Hating the bayonet and drum.

Each desperate burning brain you soothe,
Or ghastly broken frame you bind,
Brings one day nearer our bright goal,
The love-alliance of mankind.

WELLESLEY.
February, 1916.

THIRD SECTION

AMERICA AT WAR WITH GERMANY
BEGINNING APRIL, 1917

OUR MOTHER POCAHONTAS

(NOTE : — Pocahontas is buried at Gravesend, England.)

"Pocahontas' body, lovely as a poplar, sweet as a red haw in November or a pawpaw in May — did she wonder? does she remember — in the dust — in the cool tombs?"

CARL SANDBURG.

I

Powhatan was conqueror,
Powhatan was emperor.
He was akin to wolf and bee,
Brother of the hickory tree.
Son of the red lightning stroke
And the lightning-shivered oak.
His panther-grace bloomed in the maid
Who laughed among the winds and played
In excellence of savage pride,
Wooing the forest, open-eyed,
In the springtime,
In Virginia,
Our Mother, Pocahontas.

39

Her skin was rosy copper-red.

And high she held her beauteous head.

Her step was like a rustling leaf :

Her heart a nest, untouched of grief.

She dreamed of sons like Powhatan,

And through her blood the lightning ran.

Love-cries with the birds she sung,

Birdlike

In the grape-vine swung.

The Forest, arching low and wide

Gloried in its Indian bride.

Rolfe, that dim adventurer

Had not come a courtier.

John Rolfe is not our ancestor.

We rise from out the soul of her

Held in native wonderland,

While the sun's rays kissed her hand,

In the springtime,

In Virginia,

Our Mother, Pocahontas.

II

She heard the forest talking,

Across the sea came walking,

And traced the paths of Daniel Boone,

Then westward chased the painted moon.
She passed with wild young feet
On to Kansas wheat,
On to the miners' west,
The echoing cañons' guest,
Then the Pacific sand,
Waking,
Thrilling,
The midnight land. . . .

On Adams street and Jefferson —
Flames coming up from the ground!
On Jackson street and Washington —
Flames coming up from the ground!
And why, until the dawning sun
Are flames coming up from the ground?
Because, through drowsy Springfield sped
This red-skin queen, with feathered head,
With winds and stars, that pay her court
And leaping beasts, that make her sport;
Because, gray Europe's rags august
She tramples in the dust;
Because we are her fields of corn;
Because our fires are all reborn
From her bosom's deathless embers,

Flaming
As she remembers
The springtime
And Virginia,
Our Mother, Pocahontas.

III

We here renounce our Saxon blood.
Tomorrow's hopes, an April flood
Come roaring in.　The newest race
Is born of her resilient grace.
We here renounce our Teuton pride:
Our Norse and Slavic boasts have died
Italian dreams are swept away,
And Celtic feuds are lost today. . . .

She sings of lilacs, maples, wheat,
Her own soil sings beneath her feet,
Of springtime
And Virginia,
Our Mother, Pocahontas.

CONCERNING EMPERORS

I. GOD SEND THE REGICIDE

Would that the lying rulers of the world
Were brought to block for tyrannies abhorred.
Would that the sword of Cromwell and the Lord,
The sword of Joshua and Gideon,
Hewed hip and thigh the hosts of Midian.
God send that ironside ere tomorrow's sun;
Let Gabriel and Michael with him ride.
God send the Regicide.

II. A COLLOQUIAL REPLY: TO ANY NEWSBOY

If you lay for Iago at the stage door with a brick
You have missed the moral of the play.
He will have a midnight supper with Othello and his wife.
They will chirp together and be gay.
But the things Iago stands for must go down into the dust:
Lying and suspicion and conspiracy and lust.
And I cannot hate the Kaiser (I hope you understand.)
Yet I chase the thing he stands for with a brickbat in my
hand.

NIAGARA

I

Within the town of Buffalo
Are prosy men with leaden eyes.
Like ants they worry to and fro,
(Important men, in Buffalo.)
But only twenty miles away   .
A deathless glory is at play:
Niagara, Niagara.

The women buy their lace and cry: —
"O such a delicate design,"
And over ostrich feathers sigh,
By counters there, in Buffalo.
The children haunt the trinket shops,
They buy false-faces, bells, and tops,
Forgetting great Niagara.

Within the town of Buffalo
Are stores with garnets, sapphires, pearls,
Rubies, emeralds aglow, —

Opal chains in Buffalo,
Cherished symbols of success.
They value not your rainbow dress : —
Niagara, Niagara.

The shaggy meaning of her name
This Buffalo, this recreant town,
Sharps and lawyers prune and tame :
Few pioneers in Buffalo ;
Except young lovers flushed and fleet
And winds hallooing down the street :
"Niagara, Niagara."

The journalists are sick of ink :
Boy prodigals are lost in wine,
By night where white and red lights blink,
The eyes of Death, in Buffalo.
And only twenty miles away
Are starlit rocks and healing spray : —
Niagara, Niagara.

Above the town a tiny bird,
A shining speck at sleepy dawn,
Forgets the ant-hill so absurd,
This self-important Buffalo.

Descending twenty miles away
He bathes his wings at break of day
Niagara, Niagara.

II

What marching men of Buffalo
Flood the streets in rash crusade?
Fools-to-free-the-world, they go,
Primeval hearts from Buffalo.
Red cataracts of France today
Awake, three thousand miles away
An echo of Niagara,
The cataract Niagara.

MARK TWAIN AND JOAN OF ARC

When Yankee soldiers reach the barricade
Then Joan of Arc gives each the accolade.

For she is there in armor clad, today,
All the young poets of the wide world say.

Which of our freemen did she greet the first,
Seeing him come against the fires accurst?

Mark Twain, our Chief, with neither smile nor jest,
Leading to war our youngest and our best.

The Yankee to King Arthur's court returns.
The sacred flag of Joan above him burns.

For she has called his soul from out the tomb.
And where she stands, there he will stand till doom.

    •   •   •   •   •   •   •

But I, I can but mourn, and mourn again
At bloodshed caused by angels, saints, and men.

THE BANKRUPT PEACE MAKER

I opened the ink-well and smoke filled the room.
The smoke formed the giant frog-cat of my doom.
His web feet left dreadful slime tracks on the floor.
He had hammer and nails that he laid by the door.
He sprawled on the table, claw-hands in my hair.
He looked through my heart to the mud that was there.
Like a black-mailer hating his victim he spoke :
"When I see all your squirming I laugh till I choke
Singing of peace.   Railing at battle.
Soothing a handful with saccharine prattle.
All the millions of earth have voted for fight.
You are voting for talk, with hands lily white."
He leaped to the floor, then grew seven feet high,
Beautiful, terrible, scorn in his eye :
The Devil Eternal, Apollo grown old,
With beard of bright silver and garments of gold.
"What will you do to end war for good?
Will you stand by the book-case, be nailed to the wood?"
I stretched out my arms.   He drove the nails deep,
Silently, coolly.   The house was asleep,

I hung for three years, forbidden to die.
I seemed but a shadow the servants passed by.
At the end of the time with hot irons he returned.
"The Quitter Sublime" on my bosom he burned.
As he seared me he hissed : "You are wearing away.
The good angels tell me you leave them today.
You want to come down from the nails in the door.
The victor must hang there three hundred years more.
If any prig-saint would outvote all mankind
He must use an immortally resolute mind.
Think what the saints of Benares endure,
Through infinite birthpangs their courage is sure.
Self-tortured, self-ruled, they build their powers high,
Until they are gods, overmaster the sky."
Then he pulled out the nails.   He shouted "Come in."
To heal me there stepped in a lady of sin.
Her hand was in mine.   We walked in the sun.
She said : "Now forget them, the Saxon and Hun.
You are dreary and aged and silly and weak.
Let us smell the sweet groves.   Let the summertime speak."
We walked to the river.   We swam there in state.
I was a serpent.   She was my mate.
I forgot in the marsh, as I tumbled about,
That trial in my room, where I did not hold out.
Since I was a serpent, my mate seemed to me

As a mermaiden seems to a fisher at sea,

Or a whisky soaked girl to a whisky soaked king.

I woke.   She had turned to a ravening thing

On the table — a buzzard with leperous head.

She tore up my rhymes and my drawings.   She said

"I am your own cheap bankrupt soul.

Will you die for the nations, making them whole?

We joy in the swamp and here we are gay.

Will you bring your fine peace to the nations today?"

"THIS, MY SONG, IS MADE FOR KERENSKY"

(Being a Chant of the American Soap-Box and the Russian Revolution.)

O market square, O slattern place,
Is glory in your slack disgrace?
Plump quack doctors sell their pills,
Gentle grafters sell brass watches,
Silly anarchists yell their ills.
Shall we be as weird as these?
In the breezes nod and wheeze?

Heaven's mass is sung,
Tomorrow's mass is sung
In a spirit tongue
By wind and dust and birds,
The high mass of liberty,
While wave the banners red:
Sung round the soap-box,
A mass for soldiers dead.

When you leave your faction in the once-loved hall,
Like a true American tongue-lash them all,

Stand then on the corner under starry skies
And get you a gang of the worn and the wise.
The soldiers of the Lord may be squeaky when they rally,
The soldiers of the Lord are a queer little army,
But the soldiers of the Lord, before the year is through,
Will gather the whole nation, recruit all creation,
To smite the hosts abhorred, and all the heavens renew —
Enforcing with the bayonet the thing the ages teach —
Free speech !
Free speech !

Down with the Prussians, and all their works.
Down with the Turks.
Down with every army that fights against the soap-box,
The Pericles, Socrates, Diogenes soap-box,
The old Elijah, Jeremiah, John-the-Baptist soap-box,
The Rousseau, Mirabeau, Danton soap-box,
The Karl Marx, Henry George, Woodrow Wilson soap-box.
We will make the wide earth safe for the soap-box,
The everlasting foe of beastliness and tyranny,
Platform of liberty : — Magna Charta liberty,
Andrew Jackson liberty, bleeding Kansas liberty,
New-born Russian liberty : —
Battleship of thought,
The round world over,

Loved by the red-hearted,
Loved by the broken-hearted,
Fair young Amazon or proud tough rover,
Loved by the lion,
Loved by the lion,
Loved by the lion,
Feared by the fox.

The Russion Revolution is the world revolution.
Death at the bedstead of every Kaiser knocks.
The Hohenzollern army shall be felled like the ox.
The fatal hour is striking in all the doomsday clocks.
The while, by freedom's alchemy
Beauty is born.
Ring every sleigh-bell, ring every church bell,
Blow the clear trumpet, and listen for the answer: —
The blast from the sky of the Gabriel horn.

Hail the Russian picture around the little box: —
Exiles,
Troops in files,
Generals in uniform,
Mujiks in their smocks,
And holy maiden soldiers who have cut away their
    locks.

All the peoples and the nations in processions mad and
    great,
Are rolling through the Russian Soul as through a city
    gate : —
As though it were a street of stars that paves the shadowy
    deep.
And mighty Tolstoi leads the van along the stairway steep.

But now the people shout :
"Hail to Kerensky,
He hurled the tyrants out."
And this my song is made for Kerensky,
Prophet of the world-wide intolerable hope,
There on the soap-box, seasoned, dauntless,
There amid the Russian celestial kaleidoscope,
Flags of liberty, rags and battlesmoke.

Moscow and Chicago !
Come let us praise battling Kerensky,
Bravo ! Bravo !
Comrade Kerensky the thunderstorm and rainbow !
Comrade Kerensky, Bravo, Bravo !

August, 1917.

FOURTH SECTION

TRAGEDIES, COMEDIES, AND DREAMS

OUR GUARDIAN ANGELS AND THEIR CHILDREN

Where a river roars in rapids
And doves in maples fret,
Where peace has decked the pastures
Our guardian angels met. .

Long they had sought each other
In God's mysterious name,
Had climbed the solemn chaos tides
Alone, with hope aflame:

Amid the demon deeps had wound
By many a fearful way.
As they beheld each other
Their shout made glad the day.

No need of purse delayed them,
No hand of friend or kin —
Nor menace of the bell and book,
Nor fear of mortal sin.

You did not speak, my girl,
At this, our parting hour.
Long we held each other
And watched their deeds of power.

They made a curious Eden.
We saw that it was good.
We thought with them in unison.
We proudly understood

Their amaranth eternal,
Their roses strange and fair,
The asphodels they scattered
Upon the living air.

They built a house of clouds
With skilled immortal hands.
They entered through the silver doors.
Their wings were wedded brands.

I labored up the valley
To granite mountains free.
You hurried down the river
To Zidon by the sea.

But at their place of meeting
They keep a home and shrine.

Your angel twists a purple flax,
Then weaves a mantle fine.

My angel, her defender
Upstanding, spreads the light
On painted clouds of fancy
And mists that touch the height.

Their sturdy babes speak kindly
And fly and run with joy,
Shepherding the helpless lambs —
A Grecian girl and boy.

These children visit Heaven
Each year and make of worth
All we planned and wrought in youth
And all our tears on earth.

From books our God has written
They sing of high desire.
They turn the leaves in gentleness.
Their wings are folded fire.

EPITAPHS FOR TWO PLAYERS

I. Edwin Booth

An old actor at the Player's Club told me that Edwin
Booth first impersonated Hamlet when a barnstormer in
California.   There were few theatres, but the hotels were
provided with crude assembly rooms for strolling players.

> The youth played in the blear hotel.
> The rafters gleamed with glories strange.
> And winds of mourning Elsinore
> Howling at chance and fate and change;
> Voices of old Europe's dead
> Disturbed the new-built cattle-shed,
> The street, the high and solemn range.
>
> The while the coyote barked afar
> All shadowy was the battlement.
> The ranch-boys huddled and grew pale,
> Youths who had come on riot bent.
> Forgot were pranks well-planned to sting.
> Behold there rose a ghostly king,
> And veils of smoking Hell were rent.

When Edwin Booth played Hamlet, then
The camp-drab's tears could not but flow.
Then Romance lived and breathed and burned.
She felt the frail queen-mother's woe,
Thrilled for Ophelia, fond and blind,
And Hamlet, cruel, yet so kind,
And moaned, his proud words hurt her so.

A haunted place, though new and harsh!
The Indian and the Chinaman
And Mexican were fain to learn
What had subdued the Saxon clan.
Why did they mumble, brood, and stare
When the court-players curtsied fair
And the Gonzago scene began?

And ah, the duel scene at last!
They cheered their prince with stamping feet.
A death-fight in a palace! Yea,
With velvet hangings incomplete,
A pasteboard throne, a pasteboard crown,
And yet a monarch tumbled down,
A brave lad fought in splendor meet.

Was it a palace or a barn?
Immortal as the gods he flamed.

There in his last great hour of rage
His foil avenged a mother shamed.
In duty stern, in purpose deep
He drove that king to his black sleep
And died, all godlike and untamed.

.   .   .   .

I was not born in that far day.
I hear the tale from heads grown white.
And then I walk that earlier street,
The mining camp at candle-light.
I meet him wrapped in musings fine
Upon some whispering silvery line
He yet resolves to speak aright.

II. Epitaph for John Bunny, Motion Picture Comedian

In which he is remembered in similitude, by reference to
Yorick, the king's jester, who died when Hamlet and
Ophelia were children.

Yorick is dead.   Boy Hamlet walks forlorn
Beneath the battlements of Elsinore.
Where are those oddities and capers now
That used to "set the table on a roar"?

EPITAPHS FOR TWO PLAYERS

And do his bauble-bells beyond the clouds
Ring out, and shake with mirth the planets bright?
No doubt he brings the blessed dead good cheer,
But silence broods on Elsinore tonight.

That little elf, Ophelia, eight years old,
Upon her battered doll's staunch bosom weeps.
("O best of men, that wove glad fairy-tales.")
With tear-burned face, at last the darling sleeps.

Hamlet himself could not give cheer or help,
Though firm and brave, with his boy-face controlled.
For every game they started out to play
Yorick invented, in the days of old.

The times are out of joint! O cursed spite!
The noble jester Yorick comes no more.
And Hamlet hides his tears in boyish pride
By some lone turret-stair of Elsinore.

MAE MARSH, MOTION PICTURE ACTRESS

In "Man's Genesis," "The Wild Girl of the Sierras,"
"The Wharf Rat," "A Girl of the Paris Streets," etc.

I

The arts are old, old as the stones
From which man carved the sphinx austere.
Deep are the days the old arts bring :
Ten thousand years of yesteryear.

II

She is madonna in an art
As wild and young as her sweet eyes :
A frail dew flower from this hot lamp
That is today's divine surprise.

Despite raw lights and gloating mobs
She is not seared : a picture still :
Rare silk the fine director's hand
May weave for magic if he will.

When ancient films have crumbled like
Papyrus rolls of Egypt's day,
Let the dust speak : "Her pride was high,
All but the artist hid away :

"Kin to the myriad artist clan
Since time began, whose work is dear."
The deep new ages come with her,
Tomorrow's years of yesteryear.

TWO OLD CROWS

Two old crows sat on a fence rail.
Two old crows sat on a fence rail,
Thinking of effect and cause,
Of weeds and flowers,
And nature's laws.
One of them muttered, one of them stuttered,
One of them stuttered, one of them muttered.
Each of them thought far more than he uttered.
One crow asked the other crow a riddle.
One crow asked the other crow a riddle:
The muttering crow
Asked the stuttering crow,
"Why does a bee have a sword to his fiddle?
Why does a bee have a sword to his fiddle?"
"Bee-cause," said the other crow,
"Bee-cause,
B B B B B B B B B B B B B B B B-cause."

Just then a bee flew close to their rail: —
"Buzzzzzzzzzzzzzzzzzzz   zzzzzzzzz   zzzzzzzzzzzzzzzz
    ZZZZZZZZ."

And those two black crows
Turned pale,
And away those crows did sail.
Why?
B B B B B B B B B B B B B B B B B-cause.
B B B B B B B B B B B B B B B B B-cause.
"Buzzzzzzzzzzzzzzz   zzzzzzzzz   zzzzzzzzzzzzzzz
ZZZZZZZ."

THE DRUNKARD'S FUNERAL

"Yes," said the sister with the little pinched face,
The busy little sister with the funny little tract : —
"This is the climax, the grand fifth act.
There rides the proud, at the finish of his race.
There goes the hearse, the mourners cry,
The respectable hearse goes slowly by.
The wife of the dead has money in her purse,
The children are in health, so it might have been worse.
That fellow in the coffin led a life most foul.
A fierce defender of the red bar-tender,
At the church he would rail,
At the preacher he would howl.
He planted every deviltry to see it grow.
He wasted half his income on the lewd and the low.
He would trade engender for the red bar-tender,
He would homage render to the red bar-tender,
And in ultimate surrender to the red bar-tender,
He died of the tremens, as crazy as a loon,
And his friends were glad, when the end came soon.

There goes the hearse, the mourners cry,
The respectable hearse goes slowly by.
And now, good friends, since you see how it ends,
Let each nation-mender flay the red bar-tender, —
Abhor
The transgression
Of the red bar-tender, —
Ruin
The profession
Of the red bar-tender:
Force him into business where his work does good.
Let him learn how to plough, let him learn to chop
    wood,
Let him learn how to plough, let him learn to chop
    wood.

"The moral,
The conclusion,
The verdict now you know: —
'The saloon must go,
The saloon must go,
The saloon,
The saloon,
The saloon,
Must go.'"

"You are right, little sister," I said to myself,
"You are right, good sister," I said.
"Though you wear a mussy bonnet
On your little gray head,
You are right, little sister," I said.

THE RAFT

The whole world on a raft! A King is here,
The record of his grandeur but a smear.
Is it his deacon-beard, or old bald pate
That makes the band upon his whims to wait?
Loot and mud-honey have his soul defiled.
Quack, pig, and priest, he drives camp-meetings wild
Until they shower their pennies like spring rain
That he may preach upon the Spanish main.
What landlord, lawyer, voodoo-man has yet
A better native right to make men sweat?

The whole world on a raft! A Duke is here
At sight of whose lank jaw the muses leer.
Journeyman-printer, lamb with ferret eyes,
In life's skullduggery he takes the prize —
Yet stands at twilight wrapped in Hamlet dreams.
Into his eyes the Mississippi gleams.
The sandbar sings in moonlit veils of foam.
A candle shines from one lone cabin home.
The waves reflect it like a drunken star.

A banjo and a hymn are heard afar.
No solace on the lazy shore excels
The Duke's blue castle with its steamer-bells.
The floor is running water, and the roof
The stars' brocade with cloudy warp and woof.

And on past sorghum fields the current swings.
To Christian Jim the Mississippi sings.
This prankish wave-swept barque has won its place,
A ship of jesting for the human race.
But do you laugh when Jim bows down forlorn
His babe, his deaf Elizabeth to mourn?
And do you laugh, when Jim, from Huck apart
Gropes through the rain and night with breaking heart?

But now that imp is here and we can smile,
Jim's child and guardian this long-drawn while.
With knife and heavy gun, a hunter keen,
He stops for squirrel-meat in islands green.
The eternal gamin, sleeping half the day,
Then stripped and sleek, a river-fish at play.
And then well-dressed, ashore, he sees life spilt.
The river-bank is one bright crazy-quilt
Of patch-work dream, of wrath more red than lust,
Where long-haired feudist Hotspurs bite the dust . . .

This Huckleberry Finn is but the race,
America, still lovely in disgrace,
New childhood of the world, that blunders on
And wonders at the darkness and the dawn,
The poor damned human race, still unimpressed
With its damnation, all its gamin breast
Chorteling at dukes and kings with nigger Jim,
Then plotting for their fall, with jestings grim.

Behold a Republic
Where a river speaks to men
And cries to those that love its ways,
Answering again
When in the heart's extravagance
The rascals bend to say
"O singing Mississippi
Shine, sing for us today."

But who is this in sweeping Oxford gown
Who steers the raft, or ambles up and down,
Or throws his gown aside, and there in white
Stands gleaming like a pillar of the night?
The lion of high courts, with hoary mane,
Fierce jester that this boyish court will gain —
Mark Twain!

The bad world's idol:
Old Mark Twain!

He takes his turn as watchman with the rest,
With secret transports to the stars addressed,
With nightlong broodings upon cosmic law,
With daylong laughter at this world so raw.

All praise to Emerson and Whitman, yet
The best they have to say, their sons forget.
But who can dodge this genius of the stream,
The Mississippi Valley's laughing dream?
He is the artery that finds the sea
In this the land of slaves, and boys still free.
He is the river, and they one and all
Sail on his breast, and to each other call.

Come let us disgrace ourselves,
Knock the stuffed gods from their shelves,
And cinders at the schoolhouse fling.
Come let us disgrace ourselves,
And live on a raft with gray Mark Twain
And Huck and Jim
And the Duke and the King.

.

.

THE GHOSTS OF THE BUFFALOES

Would I might rouse the Lincoln in you all,
That which is gendered in the wilderness
From lonely prairies and God's tenderness.
Imperial soul, star of a weedy stream,
Born where the ghosts of buffaloes still dream,
Whose spirit hoof-beats storm above his grave,
Above that breast of earth and prairie-fire —
Fire that freed the slave.

    *   *   *   *   *   *

Last night at black midnight I woke with a cry,
The windows were shaking, there was thunder on high,
The floor was a-tremble, the door was a-jar,
White fires, crimson fires, shone from afar.
I rushed to the door yard.   The city was gone.
My home was a hut without orchard or lawn.
It was mud-smear and logs near a whispering stream,
Nothing else built by man could I see in my dream . . .
Then . . .

Ghost-kings came headlong, row upon row,
Gods of the Indians, torches aglow.

They mounted the bear and the elk and the deer,
And eagles gigantic, aged and sere,
They rode long-horn cattle, they cried "A-la-la."
They lifted the knife, the bow, and the spear,
They lifted ghost-torches from dead fires below,
The midnight made grand with the cry "A-la-la."
The midnight made grand with a red-god charge,
A red-god show,
A red-god show,
"A-la-la, a-la-la, a-la-la, a-la-la."

With bodies like bronze, and terrible eyes
Came the rank and the file, with catamount cries,
Gibbering, yipping, with hollow-skull clacks,
Riding white bronchos with skeleton backs,
Scalp-hunters, beaded and spangled and bad,
Naked and lustful and foaming and mad,
Flashing primeval demoniac scorn,
Blood-thirst and pomp amid darkness reborn,
Power and glory that sleep in the grass
While the winds and the snows and the great rains pass.
They crossed the gray river, thousands abreast,
They rode in infinite lines to the west,

Tide upon tide of strange fury and foam,
Spirits and wraiths, the blue was their home,
The sky was their goal where the star-flags are furled,
And on past those far golden splendors they whirled.
They burned to dim meteors, lost in the deep.
And I turned in dazed wonder, thinking of sleep.

And the wind crept by
Alone, unkempt, unsatisfied,
The wind cried and cried —
Muttered of massacres long past,
Buffaloes in shambles vast . . .
An owl said : "Hark, what is a-wing?"
I heard a cricket carolling,
I heard a cricket carolling,
I heard a cricket carolling.

Then . . .
Snuffing the lightning that crashed from on high
Rose royal old buffaloes, row upon row.
The lords of the prairie came galloping by.
And I cried in my heart "A-la-la, a-la-la,
A red-god show,
A red-god show,
A-la-la, a-la-la, a-la-la, a-la-la."

Buffaloes, buffaloes, thousands abreast,
A scourge and amazement, they swept to the west.
With black bobbing noses, with red rolling tongues,
Coughing forth steam from their leather-wrapped lungs,
Cows with their calves, bulls big and vain,
Goring the laggards, shaking the mane,
Stamping flint feet, flashing moon eyes,
Pompous and owlish, shaggy and wise.
Like sea-cliffs and caves resounded their ranks
With shoulders like waves, and undulant flanks.
Tide upon tide of strange fury and foam,
Spirits and wraiths, the blue was their home,
The sky was their goal where the star-flags are furled,
And on past those far golden splendors they whirled.
They burned to dim meteors, lost in the deep,
And I turned in dazed wonder, thinking of sleep.

I heard a cricket's cymbals play,
A scarecrow lightly flapped his rags,
And a pan that hung by his shoulder rang,
Rattled and thumped in a listless way,
And now the wind in the chimney sang,
The wind in the chimney,
The wind in the chimney,
The wind in the chimney,

Seemed to say : —
"Dream, boy, dream,
If you anywise can.
To dream is the work
Of beast or man.
Life is the west-going dream-storm's breath,
Life is a dream, the sigh of the skies,
The breath of the stars, that nod on their pillows
With their golden hair mussed over their eyes."
The locust played on his musical wing,
Sang to his mate of love's delight.
I heard the whippoorwill's soft fret.
I heard a cricket carolling,
I heard a cricket carolling,
I heard a cricket say : "Good-night, good-night,
Good-night, good-night, . . . good-night."

THE BRONCHO THAT WOULD NOT BE BROKEN

A little colt — broncho, loaned to the farm
To be broken in time without fury or harm,
Yet black crows flew past you, shouting alarm,
Calling "Beware," with lugubrious singing . . .
The butterflies there in the bush were romancing,
The smell of the grass caught your soul in a trance,
So why be a-fearing the spurs and the traces,
O broncho that would not be broken of dancing?

You were born with the pride of the lords great and olden
Who danced, through the ages, in corridors golden.
In all the wide farm-place the person most human.
You spoke out so plainly with squealing and capering,
With whinnying, snorting, contorting and prancing,
As you dodged your pursuers, looking askance,
With Greek-footed figures, and Parthenon paces,
O broncho that would not be broken of dancing.

The grasshoppers cheered. "Keep whirling," they said.
The insolent sparrows called from the shed
"If men will not laugh, make them wish they were dead."

But arch were your thoughts, all malice displacing,
Though the horse-killers came, with snake-whips advancing.
You bantered and cantered away your last chance.
And they scourged you, with Hell in their speech and their
faces,
O broncho that would not be broken of dancing.

"Nobody cares for you," rattled the crows,
As you dragged the whole reaper, next day, down the rows.
The three mules held back, yet you danced on your toes.
You pulled like a racer, and kept the mules chasing.
You tangled the harness with bright eyes side-glancing,
While the drunk driver bled you — a pole for a lance —
And the giant mules bit at you — keeping their places.
O broncho that would not be broken of dancing.

In that last afternoon your boyish heart broke.
The hot wind came down like a sledge-hammer stroke.
The blood-sucking flies to a rare feast awoke.
And they searched out your wounds, your death-warrant
tracing.
And the merciful men, their religion enhancing,
Stopped the red reaper, to give you a chance.
Then you died on the prairie, and scorned all disgraces,
O broncho that would not be broken of dancing.

SOUVENIR OF GREAT BEND, KANSAS.

THE PRAIRIE BATTLEMENTS

(To Edgar Lee Masters, with great respect.)

Here upon the prairie
Is our ancestral hall.
Agate is the dome,
Cornelian the wall.
Ghouls are in the cellar,
But fays upon the stairs.
And here lived old King Silver Dreams,
Always at his prayers.

Here lived grey Queen Silver Dreams,
Always singing psalms,
And haughty Grandma Silver Dreams,
Throned with folded palms.
Here played cousin Alice.
Her soul was best of all.
And every fairy loved her,
In our ancestral hall.

Alice has a prairie grave.
The King and Queen lie low,

And aged Grandma Silver Dreams,
Four tombstones in a row.
But still in snow and sunshine
Stands our ancestral hall.
Agate is the dome,
Cornelian the wall.
And legends walk about,
And proverbs, with proud airs.
Ghouls are in the cellar,
But fays upon the stairs.

THE FLOWER OF MENDING

(To Eudora, after I had had certain dire adventures.)

When Dragon-fly would fix his wings,
When Snail would patch his house,
When moths have marred the overcoat
Of tender Mister Mouse,

The pretty creatures go with haste
To the sunlit blue-grass hills
Where the Flower of Mending yields the wax
And webs to help their ills.

The hour the coats are waxed and webbed
They fall into a dream,
And when they wake the ragged robes
Are joined without a seam.

My heart is but a dragon-fly,
My heart is but a mouse,
My heart is but a haughty snail
In a little stony house.

Your hand was honey-comb to heal,
Your voice a web to bind.
You were a Mending Flower to me
To cure my heart and mind.

ALONE IN THE WIND, ON THE PRAIRIE

I know a seraph who has golden eyes,
And hair of gold, and body like the snow.
Here in the wind I dream her unbound hair
Is blowing round me, that desire's sweet glow
Has touched her pale keen face, and willful mien.
And though she steps as one in manner born
To tread the forests of fair Paradise,
Dark memory's wood she chooses to adorn.
Here with bowed head, bashful with half-desire
She glides into my yesterday's deep dream,
All glowing by the misty ferny cliff
Beside the far forbidden thundering stream.
Within my dream I shake with the old flood.
I fear its going, ere the spring days go.
Yet pray the glory may have deathless years,
And kiss her hair, and sweet throat like the snow.

TO LADY JANE

Romance was always young.
You come today
Just eight years old
With marvellous dark hair.
Younger than Dante found you
When you turned
His heart into the way
That found the heavenly stair.

Perhaps we must be strangers.
I confess
My soul this hour is Dante's,
And your care
Should be for dolls
Whose painted hands caress
Your marvellous dark hair.

Romance, with moonflower face
And morning eyes,
And lips whose thread of scarlet prophesies
The canticles of a coming king unknown,

Remember, when you join him
On his throne,
Even me, your far off troubadour,
And wear
For me some trifling rose
Beneath your veil,
Dying a royal death,
Happy and pale,
Choked by the passion,
The wonder and the snare,
The glory and despair
That still will haunt and own
Your marvellous dark hair.

HOW I WALKED ALONE IN THE JUNGLES OF HEAVEN

Oh, once I walked in Heaven, all alone
Upon the sacred cliffs above the sky.
God and the angels, and the gleaming saints
Had journeyed out into the stars to die.

They had gone forth to win far citizens,
Bought at great price, bring happiness for all:
By such a harvest make a holier town
And put new life within old Zion's wall.

Each chose a far-off planet for his home,
Speaking of love and mercy, truth and right,
Envied and cursed, thorn-crowned and scourged in time,
Each tasted death on his appointed night.

Then resurrection day from sphere to sphere
Sped on, with all the POWERS arisen again,
While with them came in clouds recruited hosts
Of sun-born strangers and of earth-born men.

And on that day gray prophet saints went down
And poured atoning blood upon the deep,
Till every warrior of old Hell flew free
And all the torture fires were laid asleep.

And Hell's lost company I saw return
Clear-eyed, with plumes of white, the demons bold
Climbed with the angels now on Jacob's stair,
And built a better Zion than the old.

.   .   .   .

And yet I walked alone on azure cliffs
A lifetime long, and loved each untrimmed vine:
The rotted harps, the swords of rusted gold,
The jungles of all Heaven then were mine.

Oh mesas and throne-mountains that I found!
Oh strange and shaking thoughts that touched me there,
Ere I beheld the bright returning wings
That came to spoil my secret, silent lair!

FIFTH SECTION

THE POEM GAMES

THE POEM GAMES

In the summer of 1916 in the parlor of Mrs. William Vaughn Moody; and in the following winter in the Chicago Little Theatre, under the auspices of Poetry, A Magazine of Verse; and in Mandel Hall, the University of Chicago, under the auspices of the Senior Class, — these Poem Games were presented. Miss Eleanor Dougherty was the dancer throughout. The entire undertaking developed through the generous cooperation and advice of Mrs. William Vaughn Moody. The writer is exceedingly grateful to Mrs. Moody and all concerned for making place for the idea. Now comes the test of its vitality. Can it go on in the absence of its initiators?

Mr. Lewellyn Jones, of the Chicago Evening Post, announced the affair as a "rhythmic picnic." Mr. Maurice Browne of the Chicago Little Theatre said Miss Dougherty was at the beginning of the old Greek Tragic Dance. Somewhere between lies the accomplishment.

In the Congo volume, as is indicated in the margins, the meaning of a few of the verses is aided by chanting. In the Poem Games the English word is still first in importance, the dancer comes second, the chanter third.

The marginal directions of King Solomon indicate the spirit in which all the pantomime was developed. Miss Dougherty designed her own costumes, and worked out her own stage business for King Solomon, The Potatoes' Dance, The King of Yellow Butterflies and Aladdin and the Jinn (The Congo, page 140). In the last, "'I am your slave,' said the Jinn" was repeated four times at the end of each stanza.

The Poem Game idea was first indorsed in the Wellesley kindergarten, by the children. They improvised pantomime and dance for the Potatoes' Dance, while the writer chanted it, and while Professor Hamilton C. Macdougall of the Wellesley musical department followed on the piano the outline of the jingle. Later Professor Macdougall very kindly wrote down his piano rendition. A study of this transcript helps to confirm the idea that when the cadences of a bit of verse are a little exaggerated, they are tunes, yet of a truth they are tunes which can be but vaguely recorded by notation or expressed by an instrument. The author of this book is now against instrumental music in this type of work. It blurs the English.

Professor Macdougall has in various conversations helped the author toward a Poem Game theory. He agrees that neither the dancing nor the chanting nor any other thing should be allowed to run away with the original intention of the words. The chanting should not be carried to the point where it seeks to rival conventional musical composition. The dancer should be subordinated to the natural rhythms of English speech, and not attempt to incorporate bodily all the precedents of professional dancing.

Speaking generally, poetic ideas can be conveyed word by word, faster than musical feeling. The repetitions in the Poem Games are to keep the singing, the dancing and the ideas at one pace. The repetitions may be varied according to the necessities of the individual dancer. Dancing is slower than poetry and faster than music in developing the same thoughts. In folk dances and vaudeville, the verse, music, and dancing are on so simple a basis the time elements can be easily combined. Likewise the rhythms and the other elements.

Miss Dougherty is particularly illustrative in her pantomime, but there were many verses she looked over and rejected because they could not be rendered without blurring the original intent. Possibly every poem in the world has its dancer somewhere waiting, who can dance but that one poem. Certainly those poems would be most successful in games, where the tone color is so close to the meaning that any exaggeration of that color by dancing and chanting only makes the story clearer. The writer would like to see some one try Dryden's Alexander's Feast, or Swinburne's Atalanta in Calydon. Certainly in those poems the decorative rhythm and the meaning are absolutely one.

With no dancing evolutions, the author of this book has chanted John Brown and King Solomon for the last two years for many audiences. It took but a minute to teach the people the responses. As a rule they had no advance notice they were going to sing. The versifier sang the parts of the King and Queen in turn, and found each audience perfectly willing to be the oxen, the sweethearts, the swans, the sons, the shepherds, etc.

A year ago the writer had the honor of chanting for the Florence Fleming Noyes school of dancers. In one short evening they made the first section of the Congo into an incantation, the King Solomon into an extraordinarily graceful series of tableaus, and the Potatoes' Dance into a veritable whirlwind. Later came the more elaborately prepared Chicago experiment.

In the King of Yellow Butterflies and the Potatoes' Dance Miss Dougherty occupied the entire eye of the audience and interpreted, while the versifier chanted the poems as a semi-invisible orchestra, by the side of the curtain. For Aladdin and for King Solomon Miss Dougherty and the writer divided the stage between them, but the author was little more than the orchestra. The main intention was carried out, which was to combine the work of the dancer with the words of the production and the responses of the audience.

The present rhymer has no ambitions as a stage manager. The Poem Game idea, in its rhythmic picnic stage, is recommended to amateurs, its further development to be on their own initiative. Informal parties might divide into groups of dancers and groups of chanters. The whole might be worked out in the spirit in which children play King William was King James' Son, London Bridge, or As We Go Round the Mulberry Bush. And the author of this book would certainly welcome the tragic dance, if Miss Dougherty will gather a company about her and go forward, using any acceptable poems, new or old. Swinburne's Atalanta in Calydon is perhaps the most literal and rhythmic example of the idea we have in English, though it may not be available when tried out.

The main revolution necessary for dancing improvisers, who would go a longer way with the Poem Game idea, is to shake off the Isadora Duncan and the Russian precedents for a while, and abolish the orchestra and piano, replacing all these with the natural meaning and cadences of English speech. The work would come closer to acting, than dancing is now conceived.

THE KING OF YELLOW BUTTERFLIES

(A Poem Game.)

The King of Yellow Butterflies,
The King of Yellow Butterflies,
The King of Yellow Butterflies,
Now orders forth his men.
He says "The time is almost here
When violets bloom again."
Adown the road the fickle rout
Goes flashing proud and bold,
Adown the road the fickle rout
Goes flashing proud and bold,
Adown the road the fickle rout
Goes flashing proud and bold,
They shiver by the shallow pools,
They shiver by the shallow pools,
They shiver by the shallow pools,
And whimper of the cold.
They drink and drink.   A frail pretense!
They love to pose and preen.

Each pool is but a looking glass,
Where their sweet wings are seen.
Each pool is but a looking glass,
Where their sweet wings are seen.
Each pool is but a looking glass,
Where their sweet wings are seen.
Gentlemen adventurers!   Gypsies every whit!
They live on what they steal.   Their wings
By briars are frayed a bit.
Their loves are light.   They have no house.
And if it rains today,
They'll climb into your cattle-shed,
They'll climb into your cattle-shed,
They'll climb into your cattle-shed,
And hide them in the hay,
And hide them in the hay,
And hide them in the hay,
And hide them in the hay.

THE POTATOES' DANCE

(A Poem Game.)

I

"Down cellar," said the cricket,
"Down cellar," said the cricket,
"Down cellar," said the cricket,
"I saw a ball last night,
In honor of a lady,
In honor of a lady,
In honor of a lady,
Whose wings were pearly-white.
The breath of bitter weather,
The breath of bitter weather,
The breath of bitter weather,
Had smashed the cellar pane.
We entertained a drift of leaves,
We entertained a drift of leaves,
We entertained a drift of leaves,
And then of snow and rain.
But we were dressed for winter,

But we were dressed for winter,
But we were dressed for winter,
And loved to hear it blow
In honor of the lady,
In honor of the lady,
In honor of the lady,
Who makes potatoes grow,
Our guest the Irish lady,
The tiny Irish lady,
The airy Irish lady,
Who makes potatoes grow.

II

"Potatoes were the waiters,
Potatoes were the waiters,
Potatoes were the waiters,
Potatoes were the band,
Potatoes were the dancers
Kicking up the sand,
Kicking up the sand,
Kicking up the sand,
Potatoes were the dancers
Kicking up the sand.
Their legs were old burnt matches,
Their legs were old burnt matches,

Their legs were old burnt matches,
Their arms were just the same.
They jigged and whirled and scrambled,
Jigged and whirled and scrambled,
Jigged and whirled and scrambled,
In honor of the dame,
The noble Irish lady
Who makes potatoes dance,
The witty Irish lady,
The saucy Irish lady,
The laughing Irish lady
Who makes potatoes prance.

III

"There was just one sweet potato.
He was golden brown and slim.
The lady loved his dancing,
The lady loved his dancing,
The lady loved his dancing,
She danced all night with him,
She danced all night with him.
Alas, he wasn't Irish.
So when she flew away,
They threw him in the coal-bin,
And there he is today,

Where they cannot hear his sighs
And his weeping for the lady,
The glorious Irish lady,
The beauteous Irish lady,
Who
Gives
Potatoes
Eyes."

THE BOOKER WASHINGTON TRILOGY

A MEMORIAL TO BOOKER T. WASHINGTON

I. A NEGRO SERMON : — SIMON LEGREE
(To be read in your own variety of negro dialect.)

Legree's big house was white and green.
His cotton-fields were the best to be seen.
He had strong horses and opulent cattle,
And bloodhounds bold, with chains that would rattle.
His garret was full of curious things:
Books of magic, bags of gold,
And rabbits' feet on long twine strings.
But he went down to the Devil.

Legree he sported a brass-buttoned coat,
A snake-skin necktie, a blood-red shirt.
Legree he had a beard like a goat,
And a thick hairy neck, and eyes like dirt.
His puffed-out cheeks were fish-belly white,
He had great long teeth, and an appetite.
He ate raw meat, 'most every meal,
And rolled his eyes till the cat would squeal.

His fist was an enormous size
To mash poor niggers that told him lies:
He was surely a witch-man in disguise.
But he went down to the Devil.

He wore hip-boots, and would wade all day
To capture his slaves that had fled away.
But he went down to the Devil.

He beat poor Uncle Tom to death
Who prayed for Legree with his last breath.
Then Uncle Tom to Eva flew,
To the high sanctoriums bright and new;
And Simon Legree stared up beneath,
And cracked his heels, and ground his teeth:
And went down to the Devil.

He crossed the yard in the storm and gloom;
He went into his grand front room.
He said, "I killed him, and I don't care."
He kicked a hound, he gave a swear;
He tightened his belt, he took a lamp,
Went down cellar to the webs and damp.
There in the middle of the mouldy floor
He heaved up a slab, he found a door —
And went down to the Devil.

His lamp blew out, but his eyes burned bright.
Simon Legree stepped down all night —
Down, down to the Devil.
Simon Legree he reached the place,
He saw one half of the human race,
He saw the Devil on a wide green throne,
Gnawing the meat from a big ham-bone,
And he said to Mister Devil:

"I see that you have much to eat —
A red ham-bone is surely sweet.
I see that you have lion's feet;
I see your frame is fat and fine,
I see you drink your poison wine —
Blood and burning turpentine."

And the Devil said to Simon Legree:
"I like your style, so wicked and free.
Come sit and share my throne with me,
And let us bark and revel."
And there they sit and gnash their teeth,
And each one wears a hop-vine wreath.
They are matching pennies and shooting craps,
They are playing poker and taking naps.
And old Legree is fat and fine:

He eats the fire, he drinks the wine —
Blood and burning turpentine —
   Down, down with the Devil;
    Down, down with the Devil;
     Down, down with the Devil.

II

JOHN BROWN

(To be sung by a leader and chorus, the leader singing
the body of the poem, while the chorus interrupts with
the question.)

I've been to Palestine.
What did you see in Palestine?
I saw the ark of Noah —
It was made of pitch and pine.
I saw old Father Noah
Asleep beneath his vine.
I saw Shem, Ham and Japhet
Standing in a line.
I saw the tower of Babel
In the gorgeous sunrise shine —
By a weeping willow tree
Beside the Dead Sea.

I've been to Palestine.
What did you see in Palestine?
I saw abominations
And Gadarene swine.

I saw the sinful Canaanites
Upon the shewbread dine,
And spoil the temple vessels
And drink the temple wine.
I saw Lot's wife, a pillar of salt
Standing in the brine —
By a weeping willow tree
Beside the Dead Sea.

I've been to Palestine.
 What did you see in Palestine?
Cedars on Mount Lebanon,
Gold in Ophir's mine,
And a wicked generation
Seeking for a sign
And Baal's howling worshippers
Their god with leaves entwine.
And . . .
I saw the war-horse ramping
And shake his forelock fine —
By a weeping willow tree
Beside the Dead Sea.

I've been to Palestine.
 What did you see in Palestine?

Old John Brown.
Old John Brown.
I saw his gracious wife
Dressed in a homespun gown.
I saw his seven sons
Before his feet bow down.
And he marched with his seven sons,
His wagons and goods and guns,
To his campfire by the sea,
By the waves of Galilee.

I've been to Palestine.
        What did you see in Palestine?
I saw the harp and psalt'ry
Played for Old John Brown.
I heard the ram's horn blow,
Blow for Old John Brown.
I saw the Bulls of Bashan —
They cheered for Old John Brown.
I saw the big Behemoth —
He cheered for Old John Brown.
I saw the big Leviathan —
He cheered for Old John Brown.
I saw the Angel Gabriel
Great power to him assign.

I saw him fight the Canaanites
And set God's Israel free.
I saw him when the war was done
In his rustic chair recline —
By his camp-fire by the sea,
By the waves of Galilee.

I've been to Palestine.
   What did you see in Palestine?
Old John Brown.
Old John Brown.
And there he sits
To judge the world.
His hunting-dogs
At his feet are curled.
His eyes half-closed,
But John Brown sees
The ends of the earth,
The Day of Doom.
And his shot-gun lies
Across his knees —
Old John Brown,
Old John Brown.

III

KING SOLOMON AND THE QUEEN OF SHEBA

(A Poem Game.)

"And when the Queen of Sheba heard of the fame of Solomon, . . . she came to prove him with hard questions." *The men's leader rises as he sees the Queen unveiling and approaching a position that gives her half of the stage.*

MEN'S LEADER: The Queen of Sheba came to see King Solomon.

I was King Solomon, *He bows three*
I was King Solomon, *times.*
I was King Solomon.

WOMEN'S LEADER I was the Queen, *She bows three*
I was the Queen, *times.*
I was the Queen.

BOTH LEADERS: We will be king and queen,

Reigning on moun- *They stand to-*
tains green, *gether stretching their hands over*
Happy and free *the land.*

For   ten   thousand
years.

BOTH LEADERS: King Solomon he had   *They stagger*
four hundred oxen.   *forward as*
though carrying
a yoke together.

CONGREGATION: We were the oxen.

BOTH LEADERS: You shall feel goads   *Here King and*
no more.   *Queen pause at*
the footlights.
Walk dreadful roads   *They walk back-*
no more,   *ward, throwing*
off the yoke and
Free from your loads   *rejoicing.*
For   ten   thousand
years.

BOTH LEADERS: King Solomon he had   *The men's*
four hundred sweet-   *leader goes for-*
ward, the
hearts.   *women's leader*
dances round
him.

CONGREGATION: We were the sweet-   *Here he pauses*
at the footlights.
hearts.

BOTH LEADERS: You shall dance round   *He walks back-*
ward. Both clap
again,   *their hands to*
You shall dance round   *the measure.*
again,

Cymbals shall sound
  again,
Cymbals shall sound
  again,
Wildflowers be found   *The Queen*
For   ten   thousand *a*   *1rs*
  years,   *gather wild-*
Wildflowers be found   *flowers.*
For   ten   thousand
  years.

BOTH LEADERS: And every sweetheart *He continues to*
             had four hundred *command the*
             swans.   *congregation,*
                                   the woman to
                                   dance. He goes
                                   forward to the
CONGREGATION: We were the swans.   *footlights.*

BOTH LEADERS: You shall spread wings *The King walks*
             again,   *backward.*
             You shall spread wings
             again,
             Fly in soft rings again, *Here a special*
             Fly in soft rings again, *dance, by the*
             Swim by cool springs *Queen: swans*
             For   ten   thousand *flying in circles.*
              years,

Swim by cool springs,
For   ten   thousand
    years.

MEN'S LEADER :   King Solomon,
                  King Solomon.

The refrain "King Solomon" may be intoned by

WOMEN'S LEADER   The Queen of Sheba
                     asked him like a
                     lady,
                  Bowing most politely :
                  "What   makes   the
                     roses bloom

the men's leader whenever it is needed to enable the women's leader to get to her starting point. All the refrains may be likewise used.

                  Over the mossy tomb,
                  Driving   away   the
                     gloom
                  Ten thousand years?"

They bow to each other — then give a pantomime indicating a great rose garden.

MEN'S LEADER :   King Solomon made
                     answer to the lady,
                  Bowing most politely :
                  "They bloom forever
                     thinking of your
                     beauty,
                  Your step so queenly
                     and your eyes so
                     lovely.

They bow and confer. The Queen reserved, but taking cognizance. The King wooing with ornate gestures of respect, and courtly animation.

These keep the roses
fair,
Young and without a
care,
Making so sweet the
air,
Ten thousand years."

BOTH LEADERS: King Solomon he had   *The two, with*
four hundred sons.   *a manner al-*
most a cake
walk, go for-
ward.

CONGREGATION: We were the sons.   *On this line,*
King and Queen
pause before the
footlights.

BOTH LEADERS: Crowned   by   the   *Pantomime of*
throngs again,   *crowning the*
audience.
You shall make songs   *On this line they*
again,   *walk backward,*
playing great im-
Singing along   *aginary harps.*
For   ten   thousand
years.

BOTH LEADERS: He gave each son four   *They go forward*
hundred   prancing   *in a pony*
gallop, then
ponies.   *stand pawing.*

CONGREGATION :	We were the ponies.	
BOTH LEADERS :	You shall eat hay again,	*They nod their heads, starting to walk backward.*
	In forests play again, Rampage and neigh For ten thousand years.	*A pony dance by both, in circles.*
MEN'S LEADER :	King Solomon he asked the Queen of Sheba,	
	Bowing most politely : "What makes the oak-tree grow Hardy in sun and snow, Never by wind brought low Ten thousand years?"	*They bow to each other, standing so that each one commands half of the stage.*
WOMEN'S LEADER	The Queen of Sheba answered like a lady,	
	Bowing most politely : "It blooms forever thinking of your wisdom,	*They bow to each other, again, with pantomime indicating a forest.*

Your brave heart and
the way you rule
your kingdom.
These keep the oak
secure,
Weaving its leafy lure,
Dreaming by foun-
tains pure
Ten thousand years."

BOTH LEADERS: The Queen of Sheba *They go to the*
had four hundred *footlights with a*
sailors' lurch
sailors. *and hitch.*

CONGREGATION: We were the sailors. *The King and*
Queen pause.

BOTH LEADERS: You shall bring spice
and ore
Over the ocean's floor, *They walk back-*
ward with slow
Shipmates once more, *long-armed ges-*
For   ten   thousand *tures indicating*
the entire hori-
years. *zon line.*

WOMEN'S LEADER: The Queen of Sheba
asked   him   like   a
lady,

Bowing most politely: *They bow to*
"Why is the sea so *each other, the Queen indicat-*
    deep, *ing the depths of the sea.*
What secret does it
    keep
While tides a-roaring
    leap
Ten thousand years?"

MEN'S LEADER: King Solomon made
    answer to the
    lady,
Bowing most politely: *They bow to*
"My love for you is *each other, then confer; the*
    like the stormy *Queen reserved, but taking*
    ocean — *cognizance, the King wooing*
Too deep to under- *with ornate*
    stand, *gestures of respect and*
Bending to your com- *courtly admira-*
    mand, *tion.*
Bringing your ships
    to land
Ten thousand years."
King Solomon,
King Solomon.

BOTH LEADERS: King Solomon he had four hundred chief-tains.

They go to the footlights with the greatest possible strut.

CONGREGATION: We were the chief-tains.

BOTH LEADERS: You shall be proud again,
Dazzle the crowd again,
Laughing aloud
For ten thousand years.

The leaders stand with arms proudly folded.

They walk back-ward haughtily, laughing on the last lines.

From here on the whole pro-duction to be much more solemn, elevated, religious.

BOTH LEADERS: King Solomon he had four hundred shep-herds.

The leaders go forward to the footlights carry-ing imaginary torches.

CONGREGATION: We were the shep-herds.

The man and woman pause at the footlights.

BOTH LEADERS:

You shall have torches bright,
Watching the folds by night,
Guarding the lambs aright,
Ten thousand years.

They wander over the stage as though looking for lost lambs, with torches held high.

MEN'S LEADER:

King Solomon he asked the Queen of Sheba,
Bowing most politely:
"Why are the stars so high,
There in the velvet sky,
Rolling in rivers by,
Ten thousand years?"

The King kneels, and indicates the entire sky with one long slow gesture.

WOMEN'S LEADER:

The Queen of Sheba answered like a lady,
Bowing most politely:
"They're singing of your kingdom to the angels,

The Queen kneels opposite the Ki___ d gives the same gesture as she answers.

They   guide   your
    chariot with   their
    lamps and candles,
Therefore they burn
    so far —
So you can drive your
    car
Up where the prophets
    are,
Ten thousand years."

MEN'S LEADER :   King Solomon,
                   King Solomon.

BOTH LEADERS :   King Solomon he kept
                       the Sabbath holy.
                   A n d   s p o k e   w i t h   *The two stand,*
                       tongues in prophet   *commanding the*
                       words so mighty   *audience.*
                   We   stamped   and   *The man and*
                       whirled and wept   *woman stamp*
                       and shouted : —   *and whirl with*
                                            great noise and
                                            solemnity.

CONGREGATION

RISES AND JOINS

THE SONG :

CONGREGATION

RISES AND JOINS

THE SONG :   . . . .   "Glory."

We were his people.

BOTH LEADERS :   You shall be wild and   *On these two lines, man and woman stamp and whirl again, gravely, magnificently.*
     gay,

Green trees shall deck
     your way,

Sunday be every day,   *On these two lines they kneel, commanding the audience.*

Ten thousand years.

King Solomon,   *Now they rise and bow to each other and the audience, maintaining a certain intention of benediction.*

King Solomon.

HOW SAMSON BORE AWAY THE GATES OF GAZA

(A Negro Sermon.)

Once, in a night as black as ink,
She drove him out when he would not drink.
Round the house there were men in wait
Asleep in rows by the Gaza gate.
But the Holy Spirit was in this man.
Like a gentle wind he crept and ran.
("It is midnight," said the big town clock.)

He lifted the gates up, post and lock.
The hole in the wall was high and wide
When he bore away old Gaza's pride
Into the deep of the night : —
The bold Jack Johnson Israelite, —
Samson —
The Judge,
The Nazarite.

The air was black, like the smoke of a dragon.
Samson's heart was as big as a wagon.

He sang like a shining golden fountain.
He sweated up to the top of the mountain.
He threw down the gates with a noise like judgment.
And the quails all ran with the big arousement.

But he wept — "I must not love tough queens,
And spend on them my hard earned means.
I told that girl I would drink no more.
Therefore she drove me from her door.
Oh sorrow!
Sorrow!
I cannot hide.
Oh Lord look down from your chariot side.
You made me Judge, and I am not wise.
I am weak as a sheep for all my size."

Let Samson
Be coming
Into your mind.

The moon shone out, the stars were gay.
He saw the foxes run and play.
He rent his garments, he rolled around
In deep repentance on the ground.

Then he felt a honey in his soul.
Grace abounding made him whole.

Then he saw the Lord in a chariot blue.
The gorgeous stallions whinnied and flew.
The iron wheels hummed an old hymn-tune
And crunched in thunder over the moon.
And Samson shouted to the sky:
"My Lord, my Lord is riding high."

Like a steed, he pawed the gates with his hoof.
He rattled the gates like rocks on the roof,
And danced in the night
On the mountain-top,
Danced in the deep of the night:
The Judge, the holy Nazarite,
Whom ropes and chains could never bind.

Let Samson
Be coming
Into your mind.

Whirling his arms, like a top he sped.
His long black hair flew round his head
Like an outstretched net of silky cord,
Like a wheel of the chariot of the Lord.

Let Samson
Be coming
Into your mind.

Samson saw the sun anew.

He left the gates in the grass and dew.

He went to a county-seat a-nigh.

Found a harlot proud and high :

Philistine that no man could tame —

Delilah was her lady-name.

Oh sorrow,

Sorrow,

She was too wise.

She cut off his hair,

She put out his eyes.

Let Samson

Be coming

Into your mind.

Printed in the United States of America.

THE following pages contain advertisements of Macmillan books by the same author.

A Handy Guide for Beggars

New Edition.   Cloth, 12mo, $1.25

" The Handy Guide for Beggars " is an introduction to all Vachel Lindsay's work.   It gives his first adventures afoot.   He walked through Florida, Georgia, North Carolina, Tennesee, and Kentucky, in the spring of 1906. He walked through New Jersey, Pennsylvania, and on to Hiram, Ohio, in the spring of 1908.   He carried on these trips his poems : " The Tree of Laughing Bells," " The Heroes of Time," etc.   He recited them in exchange for food and lodging.   He left copies for those who appeared interested.   The book is a record of these journeys, and of many pleasing discoveries about American Democracy.

This book serves to introduce the next, " Adventures While Preaching the Gospel of Beauty."   In the spring and summer of 1912, Mr. Lindsay walked from Springfield, Illinois, west to Colorado, and into New Mexico. He was much more experienced in the road.   He carried " Rhymes to Be Traded for Bread," " The Village Improvement Parade," etc.   As is indicated in the title, he wrestled with a theory of American æsthetics.   " Christmas, 1915," the third book in the series, appeared, applying the " Gospel of Beauty to the Photoplay."   The ideas of Art and Democracy that develop in the first two books are used as the basic principles in " The Art of the Moving Picture."   Those who desire a close view of the Lindsay idea will do well to read the three works in the order named.   Further particulars in the pages following.

THE MACMILLAN COMPANY

Publishers   64-66 Fifth Avenue   New York

Printed in Great Britain
by Amazon.co.uk, Ltd.,
Marston Gate.